BEIRUT

BURNING

BY

H. H.

HACHEM

DEDICATED TO ALL THOSE
THAT HAVE LOST THEIR LIVES
IN THE UNFORTUNATE
CIRCUMSTANCES THIS
BEAUTIFUL COUNTRY HAS
FACED IN THE DECADES OF
LIFE. THERE ARE NO WORDS
THAT CAN REPLACE THE HURT,
THE PAIN, AND THE TRAGIC
LOSS OF OUR LOVED ONES.
THE WORLD NOW CAN
FINALLY SEE WHAT IT MEANS
TO BE FROM LEBANON, A
COUNTRY LIKE NO OTHER,
AND WITH CITIZENS THAT
HAVE A WILL STRONGER THAN
YOU WILL EVER KNOW.

TABLE OF CONTENTS

COVER

DESIGN

BY

SOUFIANE CHOUNANI

FOUNDATION

What does it mean to know somebody who is from Lebanon? To know somebody who comes from that country and to understand what their families have seen, what their families have gone through. It is something completely different. Countless times throughout history, the people of this country have faced adversity in ways that other citizens around the world could not even fathom.

There are Lebanese citizens all over the world. In fact, there are more Lebanese people around the world living in other countries then there are Lebanese people living in Lebanon. Lebanese people all over the world make their stamp on society and they make an impact in the countries that they live in.

Nevertheless, every summer, hundreds of thousands of Lebanese people come back to the country for their summer vacations. If you take a walk through the streets of Beirut on a hot July day, you will see people that have come from all around the world to spend their summer there. People come from Brazil, Germany, Canada, America, France, Australia, and from many other wonderful countries around the world.

For many Lebanese people that have grown up outside of Lebanon, they too, cannot completely understand what is like for the people that have spent their entire lives in that country. Many of these people who visit Lebanon in the summer times, they grew up in first world countries. They grew up in countries where we didn't have the sorts of problems a country like Lebanon has had to face.

Amongst all the decades of violence and circumstances that the country of Lebanon has had to face, by a clear margin, the 1980s were probably the worst. Watching World News in the 1980s, people around the world were put to witness as to what was going on in the country of Lebanon; And how the civil war was tearing it apart.

If you were a child of the 1980s, and of a Lebanese ethnic background, you may have found yourself the subject of teasing in school. Kids would ask you about what it was like coming from a country that fired bombs back and forth at each other. Kids would ask you what it was like seeing dead bodies, if you were a kid that had been born there before arriving in the country where you were currently in.

Lebanon is a country that is not known for anything other than War. Let's be real here, any political conversation that involves the country of Lebanon would involve the talk of people dying, people suffering, and the outside world questioning the government that has run the country over the last 100 years.

Lebanon is not known as a country that has a great soccer

team, or football as it is known in most of the world. Lebanon has not produced very many athletes that have been prominent on the world stage. Or celebrities for that matter. A country like Brazil can boast of the great soccer team they have and all the great players that have represented their country. A country such as America can boast of the great basketball team they have and all the great players that have represented their country.

Other countries around the world have produced many other superstars. When we think of Argentina, we think of Diego Maradona. When we think of

Egypt, we think of Mo Salah.
When we think of Canada, we
think of Wayne Gretzky. When we
think of basketball, we think of
Michael Jordan. When we think of
music, we think of Michael
Jackson.

Lebanon has been embroiled in
controversy for decades and the
way that country stands, people
are just thinking about survival.
The resilience that these people
have his unbelievably strong. Even
when the chips are down, they
can be as patriotic as you'll ever
see. When tragedies happen, they
rise above it. And I'm not just
saying that, I have seen, I have

witnessed, and I have spoken to these people.

They're just cut from a different cloth. You cannot break the spirit of the people of Lebanon and you never will. They are just too strong, and they have been through too much. They have watched people close to them die under circumstances that we would never understand in the first world. Through all the tragedies and triumphs, this country has pulled forward and risen above anything that has hit them in the face.

Walking through Beirut in 1970, 1980, 1990, 2000, 2010, or 2020, you will encounter the same type of people. They will love you; they will accept you, and they will treat you as their own. Walk into the home of one of these people and the treatment you will receive is that of royalty. Even the poor people will offer you whatever they have to make sure your stay is comfortable.

Lebanon has a small upper class and a vast lower class, in terms of financial. There is truly little middle class in Lebanon. For the most part, you are either rich or you are poor. If you drive through the streets, or walk along the Manara coastline, you will find people begging you for money. In the first world, we see this all the time. At bus stations and train stations, homeless men and homeless women ask us for our spare change. This is quite common.

The biggest difference, however, is that in Lebanon, many of the people begging for money are children. Yes, this is the type of stuff we do not see on the news. Children no more than five- or six-years old approach you and ask for money so that they can help their families. These are children that should be in school and looking for other ways to better their lives. For many people in this country, going to school is not an option.

Walk into a Barber shop, any Barber shop across Beirut. What will you see? You will see your Barber and quite possibly a couple of his friends sitting in there and chatting. You will also see a boy, again no more than five or six years old, sweeping hair and cleaning up after the Barber is finished cutting. That is another kid that should be in school but because of their family circumstances, they are not. The $5 or $10 the child earns that day goes toward what his family needs for them to survive.

That child will eventually become a Barber. From time to time, the actual Barber will offer the child an opportunity to do a little cutting himself. The child slowly learns until the day comes when he is skilled enough, and old enough, to open his own Barber shop. So, the fact is that this Barber has basically been cutting hair since he was 6 years old. On a side note, therefore, Lebanese Barbers are generally considered the best in the world at what they do. They have been doing it since they were children, and by the time they reach adulthood, their skill set is remarkable.

The Barbers that were born and raised in Lebanon, but flee abroad at a young enough age, become the greatest Barbers that you will see in any neighborhood, in any city, and in any country in the entire world. The ones that stay in Lebanon, however, will always be poor.

The circumstances that you will see upon entering this country can be heartbreaking. A lot of people in this country live without the necessities of life that we do have in the first world. At the same time, they do not feel sorry for themselves nor do they cry about it. They deal with their circumstances and that's it.

Electricity blackouts are quite common In Beirut, in fact it is a daily occurrence. For people that live in buildings that have elevators, they have to time when they're going to be on that elevator so that they don't get stuck for four hours when the power goes out. Running water, it is something that does exist within their infrastructure, but don't drink it. If you do drink it, you will be on the toilet for a couple of days at least. These 2 reasons alone are enough for the citizens to be upset with the powers that be.

There are very few fields, and very few parks. Children play in the streets, some of them without any shoes on. I always thought that Lebanon would be a place that was full of soccer fields because everybody I knew that had grown up in Lebanon was a big fan of soccer. Upon the first time I ever visited this country, I was shocked. My first visit to that country, I spent a month there. And do you know how many soccer fields I saw the entire time I was there? I can count on one hand.

The country is small in terms of land space. Combine that with the fact that the powers that be have not built parks and fields, and you have a country where kids play soccer in the streets, dreaming of one day being the next Diego Maradona. Due to the lack of resources, however, this will never happen.

Even though soccer is a sport that is beloved in the country, Lebanon will never produce a world class player that can lead them to the World Cup. This just won't happen. The only way a world class player will come up, as an ethnic background Lebanese person, is if they grow up and train in other countries. Even at that point, that special player will likely represent the country he grew up in, not Lebanon.

Around the world, Lebanese people are looked upon as people that do come from shattered backgrounds. Lebanese people come from a place where guns and bombs are the norm. Soldiers walk through the streets fully armed and ready to give fire at a moments' notice, shall there be some reason to do so. You just can't believe what you will see if you ever visit that country. People that have grown up there and people that have visited there can tell you that it's unlike any other.

Every person you talk to has a story. You can walk into any restaurant, corner store, or clothing store. There is a good chance you can strike up a conversation with somebody that has experienced some sort of loss. It is just part of life in that country, loss. And these are people that are young.

A 21-year-old busboy working at a local hotel can tell you a story of how he lost his grand father to a senseless shooting in the streets of Beirut in the 1980s. He can talk about all the stories his family has provided him about his grand father, but due to the landscape that he lives in, he never got to be part of that life. As is tradition, especially in the Muslim side, that 21-year-old busboy likely bears the same first name his grand father had.

A 45-year-old shoe cleaner doing his work on a busy quarter in the city might have a story of how he and his brother went to war, yet only he came back. Part of his story might be the fact that it was he who should have died and his brother that should have survived. From the pain in his face and showing through his voice, you could tell this guy will never live this down.

An 84-year-old man Walking along the coastline every morning might have a million stories. He is one person that made it through all the horrible situations and circumstances that saw Beirut through all these decades. He has had countless friends and family perish for reasons that we would never understand in the first world. He could tell stories of how Lebanon was before the civil war, back in the 1960s and early 1970s. Hey can tell stories of how beautiful it was and how innocent the people were. But by looking at his face, you could easily tell that the innocence of this nation was stolen along time ago.

A 35-year-old woman who never knew her father. She has four kids and lives, along with her husband, in a small 2-bedroom apartment. Her father died while she was still in the womb, killed during the mad clashes of the 1980s. All she has of him are stories shared by her mother and a couple of old Polaroid pictures. She does not know much about the man, but her heart has always asked her "what if?"

Bachir Gemayel was the President-elect of Lebanon in 1982. He was killed when his youngest child, Nadim Gemayel, was only 4 months old. On the world stage, this tragedy was heartbreak. To this day, this man is remembered for his charisma and leadership qualities. But the story of Bachir Gemayel bears resemblance to thousands of stories with the same result. A man killed while his children were young, never getting to know the father that wanted so desperately to see them grow up.

We can't help the circumstances we are born into. In the first world, a person can be born poor and grow up to be rich. In a place like Lebanon, that isn't so easy. Things are a lot different in a country like this and opportunities afforded to people born in the first world are a lot more than the opportunities afforded in the third world. Remember the kids working in the Barber shops?

The people of Lebanon Have long been engaged under circumstances that have left them wondering if they would live or die. When life becomes like that, it is not easy to get out of bed. But the people of Lebanon continually move forward and live their lives to the fullest. This is a country of strong people and no matter what happens, no matter how many chips are down, the people of Lebanon will always rise above.

SEPTEMBER 1, 1920

Nearly 100 years to the very date of the publication of this writing, Lebanon became a state declared as the State of Greater Lebanon. Beirut became the Capital city, as it still stands today. The Ottoman Empire was formally split by this year and through the League of Nations Mandate, The British were given Palestine and Iraq. The

French were given Lebanon and Syria.

When learning of history in our school systems, both North America and Europe have a long-time frame to work with and learn from. Many countries of Europe have centuries of history to go through and learn from. In North America, Christopher Columbus was the first European credited with discovering America. So, America has a long timeframe history to learn from as well.

After the devastation of World War 1, or the 'Great War' as it was known by at that time, the world was in a mode of re-formatting. The Paris Peace

Conference played a large role in this as the world was still coming to terms with the after-effects of the greatest war in history at that time.

When Lebanon was first declared, it was named after Mount Lebanon Mutasarrifate, one of the Ottoman Empire's subdivisions. It was established by the Ottoman Empire initially in 1861 and lasted until the French Occupation began in 1918, 2 years before declaration.

If you look at all the names of the Arabic middle eastern nations, you will notice that Lebanon is the only one that doesn't truly have an 'Arabic' name. Granted, half of the population is not Muslim, but still, the name does stand out. This could have been a foreshadow to what was to come. Lebanon did become a country that was quite different than all the others in the middle east.

At that time, all surrounding areas were added to what was eventually Lebanon. In addition to Beirut, you had Tripoli, Sidon (Saida), Tyre, Baalbek, Bakaa, Rashaya, and Hasbaya to name a few. To this day, many of these areas are major summertime tourist attractions. The original territory included areas like Jounieh, which is another beautiful place that is often visited by tourists.

The French were to occupy for many years to come and a lot of Lebanon still has French influence in the modern day. Many people that live in Lebanon do speak the French language, although western influence has since changed that to a degree. With American entertainment and Hollywood, many children grow up singing songs in English and watching Hollywood movies, also in English.

100 years of history started on September 1, 1920. To think, however, that a century later Lebanon would still face adversity

in a modern time when one would think senseless death should be a reality of the past. 100 years, less 28 days, between declaration and the August 4, 2020 explosion. We will get more into this later, but the question remains, has there been progress?

The Lebanon we know of 2020 didn't exist in 1920. It took a generation for the patriotism to sink in. The families who first lived on this land continue to hold their right and family legacies in the country they built. Homes and land were passed down from generation to generation. It appears every family has a village; a place they call their own.

Aarab Salim, Baalbek, Barti, Chaaitiyeh, Damour, Fatreh, Hajjeh, Jbeil, Keyfoun, Kfar Roummane, and Qadriyeh to name a few. These villages, along with many others scattered around Lebanon, have been inhabited by families stretching through generations. They identify these villages as where they come from in Lebanon, even though many of them spend most of their time in Beirut.

From the very beginning, it has been evident that the people of Lebanon are a proud lot. When these people tell you which village they hail from, they do it in a manner that portrays proud and confident.

At the time of declaration, nobody knew what was to happen in Lebanon in the future. They didn't know there would be countless wars and strife. They didn't know there would be generations of bloodshed in the streets of its Capital city, Beirut.

There is now no documented person still alive in Lebanon today that was an adult in the year of Declaration. There is nobody that can sit you down and tell you stories of the beginnings of Lebanon and how it all started.

All that we have seen in the last 100 years, started on September 1, 1920. The declaration made a country that was to become a country of constant controversy. There has been bloodshed, war, and an extraordinarily little time of peace.

Lebanon in 2020 is 100 years in the making. September 1, 1920 was a date that should be remembered as the day the world opened to the country that would change the world.

MAY 23, 1926

On this very day, the Constitution of Lebanon was adopted. A unified Lebanese Republic was now declared, and Arabic was now the official language. It is important to note here, without going into detail, this was the point where the government was made to have equal representation between Christians and Muslims. This was a unique set-up, even in those times, when many parts of the world were governed by religious alliances.

With a split government in tow, surely it must have been a foreshadow to what the future would bring. If you look at the modern day in many first world countries, you don't see governments split by religion. Countries such as Canada and the United States have governments that are split by political ideologies.

The original Constitution of Lebanon was meant to be fair. The idea of it made sense at the time, but at some point, things were going to boil over and pressures from both sides would be set to implode. It is human nature to want more for your friends and family. Business partnerships are a prime example.

2 people entering into a business partnership are going into it 50-50. They both expect to put the same effort into it and they both expect to get the same rewards out of it. At some point, however, one of the partners, or both, will start to feel like they are getting the short end of the stick. I'm not saying that this is the exact circumstance that Lebanon was eventually to face in the civil war, but the idea is the same.

The following 3 points are the main principles of the original constitution of 1926:

1) There will be equal representation in chamber between Muslims and Christians.
2) There will be proportional and fair representation among all groups within the 2 main groups, Christian and Muslims.
3) There will be proportional representation among the regions represented.

The equal representation point we have discussed. Also, point #3 makes sense and is commonly used today to govern in the first world. The second point, however, is a point of contention. Although Lebanon was inhabited by the 2 main groups, Christians and Muslims, there were groups within the main groups.

The Muslims had 2 main sects, the Sunni Muslims, and the Shia Muslims. The Christians had the Druze and the Maronite Christians. These different sects within the groups also did not like each other. This would be a cause for major complications in future. Decision making and the political process would continually be hampered by these strained relationships.

The divides within got so intense, that even to this day, it causes hatred. It is rare to see a Sunni Muslim and a Shia Muslim marry each other. In Lebanon, even in modern day, there are many families that oppose this union. Not only that, but there is still hate to this day between these 2 sides!

Even if you go to other countries around the world, countries inhabited by Lebanese people, you will see that many of these feelings have not gone away. Sunni Muslims and Shia Muslims rarely engage in friendships, marriages, or any type of business whatsoever. This is as real today as it ever has been. Just remember the civil war was not that long ago.

As many Lebanese people exited out of Lebanon over the decades, in their new counties of habitation their children are starting to adopt a more liberal way of life. They didn't see or witness the destruction that eventually engulfed Lebanon back in the 1970s and 1980s.

Although it is rare, these days we do see younger adults who were born after 1990, as they engage the other side. By this, I mean Lebanese people of all different religious backgrounds uniting in some way. A young man living in the United States (a Lebanese Muslim) marrying a young lady (a Lebanese Christian) also living in the United States.

In a situation like this, both the young man and the young lady probably had a million headaches trying to convince their families that they were in love. Keep in mind, this is enough to tear families apart. The people of Lebanon are a proud people and they are known for sticking with their traditions and values.

Situations like this are starting to happen in the world outside Lebanon. But inside Lebanon it is much rarer. It is hard to see 2 fathers, 2 men who stood across from each other on the battleground in 1984, stand at the same wedding, watching their children unite in marriage.

The wounds of the last 100 years may last another 100 years. We just don't know. Hate can be every bit as strong as love. Only the people of Lebanon can utterly understand this and why it must be this way.

The original Constitution had to be designed this way at that time. It would be easy for us to look back and judge. Maybe there could have been a better way, and maybe some decisions could have been made to keep from what was the inevitable. But even if it were designed differently, would the results have been the same anyway?

There are always different ways to go about things. In the end, you can take 100 different paths that may take you to the same result. It can be said that there is no right way or wrong way. There is only the result that we must live with, no matter how much we want to prevent negative.

To this day, governments in Lebanon have their challenges. From the very first day in 1926, to present day, today. It will always have its challenges. As society evolves and people become more open minded, maybe things will

change. The original Constitution
was always meant to make
Lebanon a fair place to live. It just
wasn't enough to prevent the
bloodshed that came after.

NOVEMBER 22, 1943

If you were to walk through the streets of Lebanon in any year on the very date of November 22, then you are in for a real treat. This is their Independence Day. It is a day full of celebrations and fireworks throughout the country. In Beirut particularly, the night sky is full of color as the fireworks display is incredible. The spirits are high everywhere you go. Keep in mind, the people of this country are very patriotic, so a day such as this is held in high regard.

The French Mandate that began in 1920 was now over. Lebanon, as of that date, was its own nation, free to govern as they please. This was also the beginning of the national flag as we know it today. The Cedar tree on a white background, with a stripe of horizontal red above the tree and below the tree. This is one of the most beautiful flags in the world and there is meaning behind it.

Th Cedar tree itself is a common tree seen all over the country.

There are many who have their own viewpoint on the meaning of the Cedar tree. It does represent longevity and prosperity indeed. It is even mentioned numerous times in the Bible. To this point, it has been a symbol of Lebanon for generations.

The white background represents the name Lebanon, which means 'white.' It represents all that is peaceful in life. It represents all the good we have on our earth and mankind accepting the purity of it. Some see it as just a color, while others see it as sand, snow, and even the clouds. All forms have a peaceful meaning.

The 2 red stripes represent all the bloodshed that this country has endured and will continue to endure to protect itself. This is a vast difference in meaning from the white, which is on the same flag. In real life, these 2 red stripes have symbolized so much of what Lebanon is known for, blood. Perhaps another foreshadow. This flag was first accepted in 1943, before the civil war and all the ensuing clashes that have come after.

Lebanon was always intended to be a Sovereign State. It would be completely independent without compromise. There was never any plan for Lebanon to enter alignments with the west although it was to have ties politically. The west had a big hand in helping Lebanon to gain their independence, and as such, wanted to see continued progress moving forward.

Lebanon was, and still is, considered an Arab State. Although it has been religiously divided, mostly, it is part of the Arab family of countries. In fact, many citizens from other surrounding Arab countries have been known to enter Lebanon with the intention of 'partying.' They spend tons of money in Beirut as they enjoy their so-called 'best life.'

What I am about to say will likely be the most controversial statement in this entire book and may offend some people. Women that wear Hijabs in their own countries, when they come to Beirut, their Hijabs come off and they live a completely different life than the one they are accustomed to back home. They enjoy the shopping, restaurants, and various night clubs.

This isn't true for everyone, and it is quite the sin to live this way, but it is said to happen. For anyone of a deep religious mindset, this is disappointing and an unfortunate way of life. Due to the liberal mindset of Beirut, this is life in the Capital city.

As we have talked about, the proportional splitting of government was again outlined in the principles brought forward in 1943. The President would be a Maronite Christian, the Prime Minister would be a Sunni Muslim, and the Speaker would be a Shia Muslim. If you are reading this from the viewpoint of a person who was raised in the western world, you would think this a strange set-up. But this is how it was and always will be.

Lebanon will never be a country that will do away with proportional religious governments. Among all the changes that need to happen for this country to rise again financially, the proportional government alignments will not change. Does it need to change? Yes.

The financial collapse that Lebanon has gone through in recent history has been nothing short of embarrassing. Things have gotten so bad that it is difficult for people to pull their money out if they can at all. The citizens have been disappointed, and they have stood up. They want change too, and it may happen at some point, but the powers that be must change.

The biggest problem with religious proportional governments is that nobody takes accountability. It is easy to blame the other side when things go wrong. On top of that, they can turn around and blame the system, a system that they could have the power to change if they came together. "It's not my fault, my hands are tied." That is the attitude of government that most of the public sees and feels.

The public sees finger pointing from one side to the other. They don't see anyone taking blame or accepting the responsibility for all that has gone wrong. Of course, the people of Lebanon are going to be upset, they have a right to be. Until someone steps up and starts taking accountability for all that is wrong, then we will continue to see the same struggles.

Gaining independence in 1943 was a massive win for the people of Lebanon. They put their hearts and their souls into it by celebrating what they have, their country's freedom! Being that as it may, all the leaders Lebanon has had did make their efforts and their intentions were good. But it will take a collective effort to get past the turmoil and make it into a state of organized prosperity.

Past leaders have given up their lives, some to assassination, to affect change. So, I will not take anything away from them. Anyone who gives their life to their cause is worth being given the respect they deserve. The following is a list of some prominent figures in Lebanese history who have died at the hands of Assassination. Maybe not all confirmed the exact reason, but nevertheless:

Bachir Gemayel   -September 14, 1982

Rafik Hariri   -February 14, 2005

Dany Chamoun   -October 21, 1990

Kamal Jumblatt   -March 16, 1977

Fouad Jumblatt   -August 6, 1921

Riad Al Solh   -July 17, 1951

Rashid Karami   -June 1, 1987

Rene Moawad   -November 22, 1989

Abbas Al-Musawi -February 16, 1992

These are just a few of the many prominent people that have died at the hands of assassination. Involving yourself in politics in a country such as Lebanon could potentially cost you everything. It could cost you your life.

If you were to look up any of these names here presented, you will see that they all held high ranking positions within their respective associations. They did all they could to affect the necessary change in Lebanon. The only thing they all have in common is that they were all killed.

In the west, politicians don't have this worry of being killed. Unless you are the U.S. President, most politicians in the western world are relatively safe. Lebanon has shown to be a different circumstance altogether.

The price of independence can be steep. Since the beginning, the struggle has always been real and in many cases, deadly. Outsiders can look in and say what they want, but only those within this beautiful country are the ones that have had to live with the reality that is ever present, life and death.

Every year, Lebanon's Independence Day has been a ground for celebration. The streets of Beirut have been littered with patriotic love and life. It will continue to be this way well into the future, regardless of what external forces come to shake the citizens. This day will be celebrated forever.

JULY 15, 1958

The Lebanon Crisis of 1958 is a part of Lebanon's history that is not talked about much in modern historical conversations. A Full 17 years before the actual civil war started, Lebanon was on the verge of civil war for the first time in 1958!

This potential civil war was a serious threat between the

Maronite Christians and the Muslims. At that time, there were tensions rising all over the Middle East over Lebanon's ties with the west. Simply put, the Christians wanted to maintain those ties, while the Muslims did not.

At this time, the United States were involved and offered their military intervention. They ended up occupying Lebanon for 3 months until everything was settled. They ended up withdrawing once the crisis was averted.

Tensions between the Christians and the Muslims was a long-standing issue. Going back to the religious proportional governments. This was always going to be a problem and still is to this day. This is mentioned several times in this writing for the sheer meaning that it is the basis of the problem in Lebanon. A split government will never truly work, there will always be problems.

The Lebanon Crisis of 1958 highlighted the long-standing problem inside the country. For decades, you have basically had the government being pulled apart in 2 factions. The one side wanting to keep its western ties, and the other side that wants to be part of the Arab world.

If you took a trip into one of the other Middle Eastern Muslim countries, you'll see a major difference in how life is lived, as compared to Lebanon. Countries such as Syria and Saudi Arabia are very much conservative in their way of life and very 'Pro-Muslim.' There are many areas in countries such as those where religious rules are strictly enforced.

In many of those countries, women must be fully clothed, head to toe, and wearing hijab. This holds true for certain areas of those countries and they are strictly enforced. This is just one example of how life is different in Lebanon compared to the rest of the Arab world. In Lebanon, women are known to dress very liberally. Although there are still many 'Pro-Muslim' areas where you see mostly traditional clothing, Lebanon seems to change street corner to street corner.

You could be walking down the street in the Hamra district in Beirut and you will pass people of all sorts. You will see people of high religious values and you will see people of high liberal values. The Hamra district is one of the main tourist attraction districts as it is home to many modern businesses and retail as well. It can also be called a fashion hub of Beirut.

The Lebanon Crisis of 1958 told an even bigger story of how tensions would eventually rise again. It was only a matter of time and when tensions did rise again, it gave way to a civil war 17 years later, the likes we hope to never see again.

In a way, the culture of Lebanon has really been shaped by the diversity of its population. With all these differing factions of religious views, it has paved the way for a country full of open-minded people in their way of life. In the Middle East, Beirut is a city like no other. It shows in everything the country offers and how the people of the country relate to outsiders. They are very inviting to outside customs and traditions.

Between 1958 to 1975, Beirut truly put itself on the map of major international cities and tourists flocked to the Lebanon Capital. This was a period of growth and the beauty that surrounded that city was second to none.

At that time, Beirut was able to flourish and it showed. On top of that, the geography of the city could not be any better. It sits right on the coast of the Mediterranean Sea. Beautiful resorts and sandy beaches. Tropical weather, especially in the summer times. The major tourist flow during the summer times made it a city of hustle and bustle. There was always something going on.

People don't realize just how close Lebanon came to civil war in 1958. Had that happened, it would have changed the course of history. Beirut would not have become the 'Paris of the Middle East' because a civil war in 1958 would have torn it apart. And who knows how long it would have lasted! That 17-year period was when Beirut truly took form and without it, it may not have become what it did.

If you ever have a chance to visit Lebanon, one of your 'bucket list' items should be to seek out somebody old enough to remember that 17-year history (1958-1975) in Lebanon. Ask them what it was like, the tourists, the restaurants, the nightlife, and the resorts. The picture they will paint for you with their words will be one that is dramatically different than the video frames you would see on the news in the 1980s.

Their body language just might tell the whole story. The twinkle in their eye while they are remembering the good times, the times before the nightmare began. If you are lucky, they may even share private intimate details of their experiences, such as where the hot spots were, their interactions with the tourists, and how life was much simpler. 1958 could have easily been 1975.

During this time, tensions were still alive. Although nothing really happened that was enough to change that, until 1975, things were increasingly tense as time went on. As the 1960's closed and the 1970s began, those tensions were building and the inevitable seemed clear.

The outside world saw it as nothing more than rising tensions, and that cooler heads would prevail. The people on the inside saw it differently. They saw a world that was on the verge of imploding, and there was nothing anyone could do about it.

That person that you would ask about the past in Beirut. Ask them if there was any difference in the year of 1968 compared to 1973. I bet that twinkle in their eye would disappear quite rapidly. While the world on the outside didn't understand, the people on the inside knew that hell on earth was just around the corner.

APRIL 13, 1975

The 15-year civil war that killed over 100,000 people from 1975 to 1990 was an absolute regretful time in the lives of all Lebanese people worldwide. Every day, you never knew if you were going to get word of somebody connected to you that would be killed. During that time, a person walking through the wrong part of the city, or the country, could have been susceptible to death.

Getting hit with an errant bullet or walking past a car that was about to blow up, was a daily worry for the citizens of Beirut. Many people left the country, but many stayed as well. The 100,000 plus people that died, their friends and family will never live it down. The stories that these people have will just break your heart.

Take a walk with me through these streets in 1984 and you'll see nothing but carnage. Bullet holes in buildings and wreckage from bomb blasts throughout the country. Beirut itself was once known as the 'Murder Capital of the World.' There was a reason for that. Leaving your home during this period was always a risk.

Fathers would leave their home to get milk and bread for their families. They would be careful which alleys to walk through and which roads to take. Some would get caught in the crossfire, turn down the wrong street, and game over. They would not come home, ever again.

If you talk to most anyone that lived in Lebanon in 1975, they will not remember that day, April 13. There were many things that happened that led up to the beginning of the civil war. There were clashes throughout Lebanon leading up to this point. Blood was the norm by this point, and the inevitable was about to happen.

On that morning of April 13, 1975, a Church in Ain el-Rummaneh was fired upon, killing 4 people. Later that day, 30 Palestinians were killed in a bus massacre in the same neighborhood. The War was on, and it was deadly.

By the time the war had ended in 1990, the country was decimated. Years of civil unrest led to the complete destruction of what was once known as the 'Paris of the Middle East.' Such a beautiful country torn down in complete carnage. Even though lasted, it never did destroy the morale of the people. A person in 1990 was just as proud to be from Lebanon as a person in 2014.

To this day, in certain areas of Beirut, you still see remnants of the civil war and what it caused. There are still buildings with bullet holes and wreckage from bomb blasts. They did spend a lot to rebuild the infrastructure and country, but the memories don't go away. In the streets, you still see wounded men, by now in their 50s and 60s, who were fighting back in the day. Some of them missing arms, legs, eyes, etc. Their bodies may be wounded, but their souls remain strong.

For the men who fought in that war, many of them claimed they were fighting a corrupt system. They were not just fighting each other; they were fighting the powers that be. To this day, that remains the fight in Lebanon. As we will get more into this, we will find that some things never change. Allegations of political corruption remains to this day.

The entire world watched from afar as Lebanon was torn to pieces. Yes, the country was on the world stage of news, but for all the wrong reasons. The people that fought in that war are now grandparents to the people who live in that country and work to make it a better place. The only problem is that the grandchildren now are facing the same challenges now as their grandparents of yesteryear.

While we don't have the looming threat of a long-term civil war coming anytime soon, we do have political unrest that seems never-ending. The millions of Lebanese people living around the world still feel this and understand that it will take a lot for change to come and be sustained.

The scars that were given and received during this time will never be forgotten. Even as generations pass, the hurt and pain suffered at the hands of this war will stay entrenched within the very fabric of Lebanon for a long time to come.

In 2008, while in Beirut on vacation, I had a chance encounter with a photographer that had numerous photographs published by the Associated Press dating back to the late 1970s. He even pinpointed a couple of photos that I was aware of. He shared with me his take on the civil war. The photos of his that were published, they were maybe 'rated PG' at the most extreme. The photographs that never were published, those were the still frames that could not be shown to the public.

The true story on the inside was not being shown on the outside. Sure, we would see footage on the news from time to time, but the pure devastation that was caused could not be felt through the lens of a camera. This photographer told me he couldn't sleep at night. The horrors of what he witnessed was too much for him to bear.

I will never forget the tone of his voice. It felt as though a piece of his soul was missing. It had been taken from him during the dark days of the civil war. I may live my entire life and not have a conversation like this, with anyone. When your soul is torn out, it leaves an open wound that will never heal.

Of all the prominent figure assassinations that took place during this civil war, perhaps none was more evident on the world stage as much as the assassination of President-Elect Bachir Gemayel on September 14, 1982. That was the blow that truly put Lebanon in front of the world during this crisis. And it was a powerful blow.

Only a year before, John Hinckley Jr. was able to get 6 shots off aimed at U.S. President Ronald

Reagan. So, the thought of Presidential Assassinations was still on the minds of citizens worldwide. Also, this was a mere 19 years after U.S. President John F. Kennedy was assassinated.

Like all leaders before and after him, Bachir Gemayel genuinely believed that he would be able to make a difference. The job as President was well within his capabilities too. The entire world did take notice at this point, things only got worse in Beirut before they got better.

The mid 1980s was considered by many experts as the worst part of the civil war. Tensions were at an all time high as they were nearly a decade into the fighting. This gave the people a lot more history of hate to look back on. The people who lost loved ones at the hands of this war had more reason to hate and keep on fighting.

On June 1, 1987, Rashid Karami was assassinated. He was the Prime Minister of Lebanon at the time. Just like that, within a 5-year period, a President and a Prime Minister of Lebanon were killed. Just writing this is difficult to imagine, but its truth and it happened.

On November 22, 1989, Lebanese President Rene Moawad was assassinated. 3 major leaders in a span of 7 years! Surely, the governments of past and present have been criticized heavily. But the fact remains that Lebanon was a country that seemingly had targets on the backs of its elected leaders throughout the civil war. It was not an enviable position to be in.

Even though it seemed as it may never end, the people did get burned out and finally peace was restored. Enough was enough, the bloodshed had to end. The Taif Agreement was signed in 1989 and it was the first step in ending the civil war. Thankfully, not too long after, the war was over.

What happened in that 15-year civil war in Lebanon may never happen anywhere else on earth. The split governments, the divided citizens, it is just too much. Let's hope we never see another April 13, 1975 and let's hope we never see another civil war. The lasting pain this 15-year period has caused will never be forgotten.

APRIL 11, 1996

Lebanon was still rebuilding after the civil war and the memories of destruction were still evident, especially in the city of Beirut. Although it was still reconstructing, there was a lot of work yet to be done to restore it to its past eminence.

April 11, 1996 was the start of the April War between Hezbollah and

Israel. It lasted 16 days and as bad as it was, it could have been worse. There was a lot of history that led up to this moment, and an altercation like this was not surprising to those involved.

As the entire world looked on again, Beirut was about to become a war zone of destruction. Tensions between South Lebanon Muslims and Israeli Jews have always been high, and this was a point in time where something had to give.

Israel did have some participation in the civil war. Their military occupied Beirut for a period starting in the 1980s. This did not go over well with the Muslims and the spite many of them had is still felt to this day. The civilians did not want them there at all.

Even though this war lasted only 16 days, civilians on both sides had been wounded and/or killed. Soldiers met their fate as well. Civilians on both sides had also been displaced, causing more problems politically. Lebanon had over 10 times more displaced civilians than did Israel. Financially, the complete economic damage totalled nearly 1 billion dollars! Lebanon had to go through rebuilding yet again.

Tensions have always been there and with no end in site. Israel and Lebanon border each other and there are many interesting developments that happen for any travellers. For instance, if you were travelling to Israel, and your passport shows that you have been to Lebanon, then you will get turned back at the gate. The same thing would happen in Lebanon, if your passport shows that you have been to Israel, then you'll be turned back at the gate.

This may or may not be true. This may just be another story in the legend of the tensions. The fact remains, however, that there will never be complete peace between the 2 sides. In a perfect world, there would be, but our world is far from perfect.

In 1996, the people of Lebanon were ready to defend their turf. Only a few short years removed from the deadly civil war, you would think that they did not want to go through this again. Wrong. They were ready to live and die with all that came with it. Remember, these are a proud people and that is a fact that will never change.

If you walked the streets of Beirut on April 11, 1996, you would have witnessed people proud and ready to stand for their country. These people proudly waved their flags, the beautiful Cedar tree in the middle. If they had to die, then they had to die. Don't you ever underestimate the heart of a Lebanese citizen!

If you walked through the streets of Beirut on April 27, 1996, you would have witnessed people proud and ready to stand for their country. This sentence is not double typed. Even after going through more guns, rockets, and bombs, their strength never waned.

I have visited the town of Nabatiyeh many times. This was where 9 civilians were killed in a building that was rocketed. The very first time I visited; I was given a tour of the area. Although I vaguely remember, I believe I did visit that site. I also remember that speaking English was frowned upon in that area. Keep in mind that this is an area that is loaded with proud Muslims that hated U.S. and Israeli enforcement.

Only a short time before this war, 4 years, Hassan Nasrallah took over leadership of the Hezbollah forces after the previous leader, Abbas Al-Musawi, was assassinated. He is loved and respected among many in south Lebanon, and this was the first test of his leadership. It truly put him on the map on the world stage at this time.

Regardless of how the west feels about the Hezbollah, an

organization can only be as strong as its leader. And while the motives of the Hezbollah may be insufficient to countries of the west, it is interesting to note that the strong leader they have has been standing in charge since the early 1990s. In the middle east, men who hold power in any form generally don't last. They are either driven out of office or assassinated.

Israel also has had problems with many other nations in the Middle East. It has been well documented even dating back to well before the 6-day war of 1967. Even in 1996, Hamas claimed responsibility for suicide bombs that exploded in Israel in February of that year.

The mid 1990s in general was supposed to be a time of peace and love. For the most part, in Lebanon, it was. But there were times, such as the April War, when the violence erupted again. Yet another foreshadow, because 2006 brought an even bigger altercation that we will get into later in this writing.

The Qana Massacre that took place on April 18, 1996 was the most senseless circumstance of them all during this April War. Let's be real here, every single death in that time was horrible. You can't help but feel for all the families and victims alike. Israel fired at a United Nations compound that was a temporary home to nearly 1000 Lebanese civilians that had nowhere else to go.

Over 100 innocent Lebanese civilians lost their lives that day and over 100 others were injured. Regardless if this was intended or not, wars bring about these situations where the innocent get caught in the crossfire. To this day, nobody has been brought to justice over this deadly massacre, and sadly, nobody ever will.

Like it or not, someone had to make that call. Someone ordered the attack. But just like so many other issues at hand in the Middle East, nobody will step up and take blame. There were investigations and lawsuits, but all with no conclusion. There was a United Nations report that said Israel knew what they were doing when the attack transpired, and it was on purpose. Wow, big fucken deal! The bottom line is that nobody ever accepted blame, that's it.

This is the problem with tension filled areas of the world, most notably the Middle East. Casualties of war are a harsh reality when it comes to tension within countries or with neighboring countries. Even more unfortunate, is the fact that events like the Qana Massacre have occurred all over the world, and with the same results. The results being that nobody took responsibility for the damage and destruction caused.

Senseless massacres like this must stop! But this is the real world, and these events will not stop. These events will continue for as long as mankind fights each other. On the other side of the world, in a society far different than the one in the middle east, our heartache stops once we turn off the news channel.

For the people in Lebanon that have had to deal with this

unshakable movement of life and death, it is real. It is very real. 1996 was very real. Had things not been handled and smoothed over, there could have been a war that would still be lasting to this day!

By the time the April War had ended, the picking up of the pieces had begun yet again. Although another war event was over, the hate continued. The people of South Lebanon and the people of Israel will just never get along. That just is what it is.

MAY 25, 2000

Liberation Day! This was the very day in the year 2000 when Israel withdrew their forces from South Lebanon. They were there for 15 years and so it is a major Holiday in Lebanon. It is one of the most important days in Lebanon's history.

It is said that one of the main reasons for its withdrawal was the constant pressure put on by Hezbollah. The Hezbollah is the best trained militia in the world. As such, it is highly believed within South Lebanon that Israel wanted no more part of Hezbollah and the constant pressure that was being put on their soldiers. I'm sure you would get a different viewpoint on this matter from the people of Israel. Nevertheless, the Hezbollah is no joke, these guys are serious, and they can be extremely dangerous standing up in the face of threat to their people.

Lebanese citizens worldwide were thrilled with the Israeli withdrawal and saw it as a great victory for the country. Hezbollah were heroes in the face of this circumstance and Hassan Nasrallah added to his reputation of being a strong leader.

In some parts of Lebanon, and within some families, this is a bigger celebration than Independence Day. Some citizens found it downright humiliating that their land was being occupied by a Jewish nation. That is not being short about it, that's just a fact. The people of Lebanon are a proud people and there is no question that this occupation by Israel burned their hearts.

Although Israel was gone, the dispute of the Shebaa farms

remained. In fact, this remains a point of contention to this very day. Lebanon contends that this land belongs to them. The United States recognized this land as annexed to Israel in 1981. Lebanon has refused to acknowledge this ever since, and they will never acknowledge it.

However, since the May 25, 2000 withdrawal of Israel overall, the Patriotism in Lebanon grew exponentially. In the early 2000s, tourism hit all time highs as many people who grew up in Lebanon came back to visit and make Lebanon a part of their lives once again. People that had left in the war-torn 1980s had finally come back and were ready to fall in love with their country once again.

I left Lebanon as a child in the 1980s. I came back for the first time in 2002 and I couldn't believe what I was seeing. Life was going on as usual. People were interacting with each other, Muslims, and Christians alike. Life had gone on post-war as this was now a full 12 years after the end of the civil war and a full 2 years after the withdrawal of the Israeli forces.

I was able to go wherever I wanted to in Beirut and South Lebanon as well. The people were friendly and there was no discontenting people anywhere I went. Everyone was living it up, restaurants were packed, nightclubs, and retail outlets were bursting at the seams, no pun intended. Going into South Lebanon, however, there was a checkpoint outside Saida, a town about an hour south of Beirut. It is the hometown of Rafik Hariri, the former Prime Minister. That was probably the only thing I saw out of the ordinary. That was, until I was about 2 weeks into my trip.

This was July 2002, and a bomb exploded in an American Franchise Restaurant in Beirut. It made the news, but it was a rather small incident compared to what was the norm in Lebanon over the previous 2 decades.

From then on, there were 2 armed military guards stationed at the door of every American franchise restaurant across the country. You name it, they were there, and they carried loaded rifles. McDonalds, Sonic, Hardees, KFC, etc....

Imagine taking your family to McDonalds and having to walk by a fully armed guard carrying a loaded gun. I honestly thought that all those restaurants would be empty, but I was wrong. Business went on as usual. All American Franchised Restaurants stayed busy. I have mentioned already about the strength of the Lebanese people. It would take a lot to jar their hearts. They don't get scared.

The Beirut of 2002 was a much different Beirut than that of 1990. The 2002 version was a gorgeous place filled with love and good times. People didn't openly talk about the war unless you asked them directly. Even then, they would tell their stories in a very painful manner, because everyone experienced loss in some way.

The early 2000s were a wonderful time in Lebanon, especially in Beirut. Everyone was enjoying themselves; everyone was making money; ultimate tourism had returned. The innocence lost in the previous generation was alive and well in this generation. The summer times were full of weddings too! You couldn't drive more than 2 blocks without seeing brides and grooms posing for pictures.

People that were around during the 1960s and early 1970s could see a resemblance of the Beirut that once was a magical place full of love, laughter, and the best life you can imagine. If the civil war made Beirut 'hell on earth,' the new and true Beirut was indeed 'heaven on earth.'

This is the only city in the entire world that can lay claim to both titles. I challenge anyone to bring forth a more deserving city. On the front end, no city wants to be known as 'hell on earth.' But every city wants to be known as 'heaven on earth.' At its best, Beirut has no peer. This takes nothing away from any other great city in our world. But Beirut is Beirut, and it always will be Beirut.

Some of the most extraordinary times came along the Manara coastline at night. Lovers of all ages would come down to this area and just walk. Young lovers would find their souls connecting while enjoying the general splendor that was around them. Couples married 50 years would rediscover their love for each other. This is a place where time stands still, it truly feels that way. There is no experience you will ever have travelling that can touch this. These are the moments you want to stand still forever.

The restaurants that you find along this area of Lebanon are amazing places to dine. Places such as 'Bay Rock Café' had been around for a long time. The early 2000s brought them even more popularity as the tourism boom had more people returning to Lebanon than ever before.

Liberation Day was a much-needed breath for the people of Lebanon, and it allowed for much needed growth. It allowed the country to be a country again and for the people to flourish. The freedom to build the country back to prominence was taking shape and the human spirit lived loud and proud.

Was this going to last? How long until the bottom would fall out again? How long until tensions would boil over? How long would this time of peace last? A beautiful time it surely was. But it wasn't long after when Beirut would make international headlines again. And again, for all the wrong reasons.

FEBRUARY 14, 2005

Rafik Hariri. This man's life ended on this very day, along with 22 others. A bomb contained in a parked vehicle, beside where he was driving, exploded near the St. George Hotel by the Manara. This killing sent shockwaves throughout the world as many thought the worst of Beirut's days were in the past. This unfortunate occurrence showed that the entire country of Lebanon is always on the brink of tragedy. For Rafik Hariri and everyone else killed in this explosion, this was tragedy.

For a few years after this happened, a memorial was set up at the site of the explosion. It became a popular tourist attraction as well. In the first couple of years after it happened, the area was remarkably busy with visitors. Eventually, the numbers waned. The memorial is no longer present at that site.

Rafik Hariri was a long-time businessman who had a reputation for giving back. He sank millions of dollars of his own money back into Lebanon during its civil war. Like all public figures, he had his lovers and his haters. Those who opposed him felt that he had his own agenda. While those that loved him appreciated his giving back.

Before he ever entered politics, he was a well-known figure in Lebanon. He wanted to involve himself more and more, especially seeing how the civil war tore the country apart. By the end of this civil war, he was heavily involved in the organizing of the TAIF agreement, which signalled the end of the fighting soon after. A statement like this might sound controversial, but it's odd to think that this man was never considered for the Nobel Peace Prize. Love him or hate him, an argument can be made.

By 1992, he had become Lebanon's first Prime Minister post-war. At this point, he set about reconstructing the country inside out. His business background came in handy as the country was slowly building itself back up again. He wasn't the only person that had a hand in the rebuilding process. The entire country was behind it and everyone played a vital role. From the politicians at the top, down to the street vendors on the corner, everyone was involved.

In the lead up to the post-2000 era, this was the time when the pieces were put in place. At this point, the country had to work together to make the change happen, and they did. Rafik Hariri led a Lebanon of the 1990s that was in recovery. There was a lot of work to be done and the Prime Minister wanted to be part of it.

He was also the finance minister at that time, and some of his detractors blame him for all the debt the country has to this day. But that was a time in that country when they didn't have many options in terms of securing the money needed. Hariri did what he had to do for progress to be made. Could someone else have done a better job? Possibly, but he was present and ready to act, nobody else was.

He supported foreign investment. To this day, many of the businesses you see in Beirut were ushered in during this period of the 1990s. Even when you walk through the city of Beirut today, you see retail and restaurants that bear international brands. This all started after the civil war and the footprints of that timeframe are still alive and well in the city today.

He left office in 1998 but returned in 2000. During this second term is when the country truly started to flourish. The effects of the development that was started in the early 1990s was truly starting to show in major ways. International business was flocking to Beirut and development was taking shape. Real Estate values were starting to see some improvement and cranes were evident all over the city. Highrise buildings were starting to replace the rubble that sat empty for decades. Foreign investment was apparent everywhere you went.

Since Lebanon is a country where the population of its own citizens worldwide outnumber the country population by 7 times, there was plenty of money that would come in for some sort of business investment. Around the world, Lebanese people are known as savvy businessmen. They make their wealth in their country of habitation but by the turn of the century, a lot of them saw fit to bring their money to Lebanon.

The Hariri-led early 2000s really did the country good in many ways. Beirut was back on top of the world as a destination city. It again became a city like no other where tourists would come for an experience, an experience they would not get anywhere else.

The day Hariri was killed was another day in the long line of sad days for Lebanon. He was killed in the heart of the city he helped to rebuild, Beirut. Even at a time when we thought the assassinations would stop, this happened. Modern protection of our leaders is at an all-time high, so this one was a surprise.

Nobody has gotten close to any U.S. President since Ronald Reagan in 1981. Hassan Nasrallah has been the Leader of Hezbollah since 1992. Ali Khamenei of Iran has been in power since 1981. King Abdullah the 2nd has overseen Jordan since 1999, as well as Vladimir Putin of Russia since that same year. Bashar Al-Assad of Syria since 2000. Khalifa Bin Zayed Al Nahyan of the United Arab Emirates since 2004. Mahmoud Abbas in Palestine since 2005.

All of these and many more leaders around the world have survived. So, with more sophisticated security systems in place, why Hariri? How did they get to him? Why did they get to him? He wasn't part of the civil war! To this day the question remains as to who is responsible.

The fingers will continue to point. There is no denying that. Regardless of who was responsible, it is something that is regrettable. Just like all the leaders of Lebanon before him. It is almost considered a death sentence in Lebanon when entering public office. This is an incredibly sad reality that affected some of our leaders of the past. The ultimate price is death.

In the same year he was killed, the airport was named after him in Beirut. You hear his name spoken on the sound system when you arrive, "Welcome to Rafik Hariri International Airport." They mention it throughout the day and his name is plastered everywhere.

The spelling of his name has always been a point of question.

In this writing, I spell it 'Rafik,' with a 'k.' In some places it is spelled 'Rafic.' For some reason, mainstream media has always been split on the correct spelling of his name. When translating names from Arabic, the different order of letters sometimes causes this.

I have known people that are related, and yet they spell their last names differently. This is due to how they applied to come into their country of current habitation. I have even known brothers that spell their last names differently! If you look up Hariri, you will see that his name is spelled differently in many publications.

In the time since his passing, Rafik Hariri's son, Saad Hariri, has blazed his own trail in Lebanese politics. In the Middle East, it is almost customary for the oldest son of a major politician to follow in his father's footsteps. We Saw it with Bachir Gemayel and his son, Nadim.

This is a remarkably similar cause to 'taking over the family business.' Lebanese people are immensely proud and will stop at nothing to protect the legacy of their family patriarch. The oldest son has an obligation to take command and take care of the family when his father dies. In the case of political leaders like Hariri and Gemayel, their sons had to assume responsibility for citizens their fathers served.

Like all the assassinated leaders before him, and the ones after, Rafik Hariri knew what he was getting into before he signed up. He knew that his life would be in jeopardy at some point, yet he had done what he had to do. To him, and all the leaders who perished in this way, they all went out fighting, fighting for what they believed in. They wanted to fight for their people, the people of Lebanon. They cannot be faulted for that. They are heroes to their families and to their people, and that will always be.

Even though there is an entire chapter dedicated to Rafik Hariri, this doesn't mean that his death was the worst of them all. All of the assassinations were unfortunate. His came at a point in time when it was least expected.

JULY 12, 2006

Here we go. The 2006 Lebanon War (Between Hezbollah and Israel) erupted On July 12 in what was said after Hezbollah fighters ambushed Israeli soldiers and took 2 of them hostage. After back and forth demands that went unanswered by both sides, Israel had no choice but to start airstrikes on Southern Lebanon. Hezbollah continued to fire rockets into Northern Israel, and the battle was on!

Cross border attacks between Lebanon and Israel were nothing new historically. Hezbollah and Israel have a long-standing hatred for each side, and this July 12, 2006 incident was the fuel that lit the fire for something bigger, and more deadly.

Yet again, Lebanon was back on stage, making headlines around the world. Due to its history of warfare, the outside world paid attention and it was thought that this war would last an exceptionally long time. Hezbollah was looked upon as the villain, especially in the west. They had started this mess and now people were dying.

It's no secret that the United States considers Hezbollah to be a terrorist organization. That may or may not be true, it depends on who you ask. Most Americans would agree with the fact that Hezbollah is a Terrorist organization. The people of South Lebanon, however, viewed Hezbollah as heroes. From the beginning until the end of this conflict, in Lebanon they were heroes.

Throughout the entire 34-day war, Hezbollah was the 'knight in shining armour' for the people of Lebanon. They were fighting for the people of Lebanon, and they made no secret about this. The people of Lebanon were proud to be at war and defending their land against the villain they saw, Israel.

Outside of Lebanon, countries all around the world had citizens vacationing in the country. Remember, this was the middle of July, high season for Tourism. Kids were out of school and their families were in the country.

Countries from around the world had to get their citizens out of Lebanon as soon as possible! Foreign nationals were everywhere across the country, and they had to get out! Of all major countries, Italy got their ship to Lebanon first, and they got their citizens out.

The problem now, however, was that other countries that were late getting their ships to Lebanon were facing heavy criticism back in their home countries. Canada was a perfect example here. At that time, Canada had over 40,000 foreign nationals in Lebanon, an astronomical number, and they needed to get out!

Canada's ships did not arrive and start taking citizens out until July 20, 2006, a full 8 days after the war broke out! Stephen Harper was the Prime Minister of Canada at that time and he was under immense pressure to get this right. While other countries had arrived and taken citizens out, Canada was 'slow' as they were labelled in the media.

People all over Canada were upset because they had family members that were waiting to leave. It is important to note, however, that Canada had more foreign nationals in Lebanon than any other country, besides Sri Lanka. This meant that their organizational efforts had to be that much more precise. So that may have been a reason why it took so long, but the people of

Canada did not care about those details, they were upset.

Eventually, citizens from most countries were evacuated and that was one less headache at the time. The ships came and went, while the fighting raged on. Attempts to broker peace raged on as well, but there seemed no end in sight as July wore on.

The fighting was heavy, and it was aggressive. One of the lasting memories that I recall was watching Anderson Cooper reporting out of Israel during an attack. He was in a van with other civilians 'chasing Katyusha rockets' as they were hitting parts of Northern Israel. He and his associates were looking to help the injured. This just may have been the single greatest piece of reporting in the history of News TV.

At the time, Anderson Cooper was considered by many as the greatest news reporter in the world. This piece he did on the rockets truly showed what the people of Israel were living through. It mirrored, almost exactly, the streets of Beirut during the civil war of 1975-1990.

Civilians on both sides were in direct line of fire, and the world was watching it on TV. That segment of reporting by Anderson Cooper showed the world what the people inside both countries were dealing with. The world was at attention and this time, the cameras were catching everything.

If you look back at old news stories about the civil war in Lebanon, you will notice that much of the interviews were conducted outside the hours of fighting. By 2006, the cameras were rolling, and we never knew what we were going to get once we turned on the news.

Israel has a strong army, so this entire clash with Lebanon should not have lasted long. But remember, the Hezbollah is the best trained militia in the world.

They are number 1, by a clear margin, there is not an organization in the world that can touch them in terms of skill. The fighting was very intense and the Guerilla Warfare that Hezbollah had deployed was effective.

As the fighting dragged on, the outside world wanted peace. Watching Lebanon go through another wartime meltdown was just too much to handle for many citizens around the world. The United Nations had to get involved, and they did. A ceasefire was developed and eventually adopted by both sides after 34 days of pure hell.

Israel could only do so much. Hezbollah was not going away. There was no way Hezbollah was going to accept defeat. All their soldiers would have to die on the battlefield for them to ever accept defeat as part of their vocabulary. Even then, Israel would have to kill all citizens of Lebanon too.

Thankfully, this entire situation concluded on August 14, 2006, when the ceasefire was agreed to. Israel had to leave Lebanon, and Hezbollah got all the credit. The way this war ended was not a good look for Israel. Some experts compared this to America's Vietnam. In that war, the United States were fighting Guerilla warfare and battling against the elements in that country. It was an unpopular war towards the end.

In Israel, this was not a popular war. In Lebanon, it was. The outcome was well received as the look was simple. Israel had 'retreated' to their country. This was the first and only time that Israel was on the receiving end of punishment just as good as they were giving it. The optics here suggested that the Hezbollah won. While that was never the case. The truth is nobody won.

Some of the spiritual people had great stories of human spirit and strength. One story stood out

among all others. A Hezbollah
fighter that was under attack. He
and his 4 comrades fought as well
as they could. He was yelling
behind him, to get help from the
other 4 men. He turned around
and saw that they were all dead.
His fate was next, and all he could
do was pray.

As he prayed, bullets flew past
him. Then, miraculously, bullets
were coming from behind him,
towards the direction of those
attacking him. He turned around
again, and this time he witnessed
all 4 comrades shooting their guns
at the opposition and fighting
with all their strength. He joined

them in shooting, and they did not stop.

Together, all 5 of them fought and killed their opposition for that day. It was a miracle and it was God's will. He then turned around again and saw all the other 4 fighters, dead. For them, it was God's will too. His life was not to end that day. His purpose had not yet been filled, yet he was ready to die for his cause. His 4 comrade's bodies were not alive, but their spirits were. I wish to meet this man someday.

Circumstances like this one cannot be explained. How Hezbollah was able to 'drive' Israel out of their country, cannot be explained. There are other stories like this one, but you may never hear them. The best chance to do so is to walk through South Lebanon and ask the elderly. They may or may not tell you.

Once the war ended, the ruins were evident. The rebuild had just started and certain areas were guarded by Hezbollah. An interesting thing to note, these men were boys. No more than 18, 19 years old. These were the guys fighting in this war! It is hard to believe that you had kids as young as this fighting a war that had to be fought. It has been said that a man of Hezbollah has the heart of a lion. They just don't back down.

If you were to visit one of these sites, you were not allowed to take pictures. If you were to pull out a camera, the guy watching the site would approach you and tell you to put the camera away. This was 2006, so it was basically just at the beginning of the camera phone era and as well, people were just beginning to use their cell phones for social media. So there likely isn't much documentation of the carnage that was, only what we saw on TV.

Buildings were partially knocked down, if not, then entirely knocked down. Bridges were taken out. Commercial plazas were ruined. Roads were turned into rubble in many areas of the south. The country looked like a place that had endured a years' worth of fighting, not just 34 days.

The scary truth about seeing these images is that these were areas that were heavily populated. These buildings, roads, and bridges that were bombed, they were in areas where civilians lived! This war was a lot more dangerous than what the outside world saw.

This war brought back old memories of a Lebanon that was entrenched in warfare throughout the civil war era. The people that lived through the civil war were now seeing life the same as it was back then, bloodshed and rebuilding. It also ushered in a new generation of experience. The young people that never experienced the civil war and all that it had done to Lebanon, particularly Beirut.

These young soldiers who were 18, 19 years old at the time, were born in the late 1980s. They were too young to remember what happened in the time before they were old enough. If one of these kids was born in 1987, then they would have been 3 years old when the civil war ended, too young to know. But their parents and grand parents knew, and remembered, and made sure these kids knew how it was.

The innocence of Lebanon had been taken again. The city of Beirut was also hit hard, as there were many areas that needed help, families that were left homeless again. Displacement has become norm generation over generation. People there now don't like talking about this war, just as they don't like talking about the civil war. When prodded, they will talk. But it serves as a cold reminder that the tension in that part of the world could unravel at any time.

Generational hate is a term not normally associated with modern linguistics. But in Lebanon, generational hate has become part of the life there as this war brought a new generation of lost innocence and extreme violence that the outside world will never know.

In the years since this war, the redevelopment of Beirut has continued. At any one time if you drive through the Capital city you will see no less than 300 cranes in different areas, north, south, west, and east.

You will see few cities around the entire world that show this sort of development post-2008. The world economic meltdown put a major hit on major development in major hubs around the world, but not Lebanon.

In fact, real estate values increased trifold after the war. It was an amazing resurgence, people started to love life again and it showed with their investment in the country. The economic and financial focus in Lebanon was on the rise again, but would it sustain over time? Just like in the movies as in real life, fairy tales don't always last forever.

OCTOBER 17, 2019

The meltdown of the Lebanese economy, sad. After 2 decades of bright development and robust tourism (Other than the War of 2006), the people of Lebanon had enough. There were protests starting across the country, particularly in Beirut. The people feel that the government is full of corruption and self-serving politicians.

The country itself has daily power outages and has had them since the 1970s. You can't drink the tap water at all. The garbage disposal infrastructure has had its share of issues as well. There are truly little work opportunities upon finishing school, unless you are related to someone who has the pull to get you a job.

There is just too much not happening for the citizens of Lebanon. The elite remain the elite, and the poor stay poor. It is exceedingly difficult to come up in an economic environment such as this and overcome the inferiority of your birth. This is unfortunate but true.

The citizens have accused the government of ultimate corruption over the years. They line their own pockets and give opportunities to their own family members. This is no way to run a country. All of these are only accusations, but you must wonder if there was nothing suspicious truly going on, then why are the people revolting?

Back in 2000, a 20-year-old man could have opened a barber shop and it would be the start of his adult life. Within the next 2 years he would marry and have his first child. He is great at what he does, and everyone sees him as someone that will become extraordinarily successful.

Every day would be a busy day at his barber shop. People from the neighborhood would stop in and talk, engaging in general barber shop banter. Kids would show up asking to work for him. Tourists from outside the country would get their haircut by him. They would tell him that he should leave Lebanon and put his skills to use in a country that can make him wealthy. He's the next big thing in the neighborhood.

Fast forward to 2019, or 2020. This barber is still working out of his same shop, seeing the same customers every day. His demeanor has changed. He isn't the same glowing man at 40, as he once was at the age of 20. He is more negative and engages into negative conversations about the government.

On a personal level, he now is a father of 3. He and his wife and children live in a small 2-bedroom apartment, that they rent. They rent because he was unable to financially purchase a home for his family. He has not gotten ahead; he has not fulfilled his potential. He hates life and you can feel it in every word he says.

Meanwhile, his friends have moved out of the country, they left when they were young. They have come back with pockets full of money, families of their own, with their kids wearing designer clothing. They come back to get their haircut from their old friend. They trade stories of life and their children, and by the end of the day, he closes shop. While he is sweeping up hair and cleaning, he can't help but wonder what might have been.

As a young man, he had the opportunity to leave Lebanon in search of more out of life. He chose to stay. He stayed because he had faith that things would eventually change and he would engage the same opportunities within this country, the opportunities his friends had in other countries.

The opportunities never came and by the time he had his second child, he was stuck. The government was not going to help him, he was on his own with his young family. Now with 3 kids, he can only wish that they take advantage of opportunities that come their way. He squandered his opportunities by believing in the government and changes that would come. Instead, he got punched in the throat by life, and he was hit by the reality that he will never live the life he desired.

In October of 2019, the protests began, and they were in full force.

Vandalism and firebombs were part of demonstrations that showed the upset nature of the people. Things got quite dangerous and people died. Albeit this wasn't like any wars they had previously. Casualties were relatively small, but they were there. Even one death would have been one death too many. Regrettably, there was more than one death and that made this a tragedy.

The people now wanted to be heard and they felt that this was the time. In years past, it would have been a scary experience to protest in such a way against the government in Lebanon. Soldiers walk around with rifles all over Beirut. You never want to be involved in a protest where there are soldiers present with itchy trigger fingers.

In the modern day, however, it has become safer for the people to rise and fight for their rights and beliefs. Had Lebanon finally turned the corner and now ready to accept change? Saad Hariri stepped down as Prime Minister.

Even though this situation had gotten out of hand, the protests itself were different than the social problems that existed before. In the past, rallies and protests were religiously divided, or even regionally divided. In these protests, Christians, Druze, and Muslims stood next to each other and protested a common enemy, the government!

This was the first time in Lebanon's history that the people united for a cause that wasn't divided by religion or political sect, or any other reason for that matter. The people have always been divided. A good example of this is the split government alignment. The country has been split for generations. People of different religious sects do not interact with each other on a common basis.

October 17, 2019 marked a shift in the gap between all sects of

Lebanon as the people united in their cause for change. The people that stood next to each other, their grandfathers and great grandfathers stood across from each other on the battle grounds. It could very well have been that their grandfathers exchanged direct gunfire.

Now, this new generation was standing side by side, obliterating past rivalries for the nature of the common good. The protests of 2015 had some common relation to the 2019 protests, in terms of united people. But the difference is, in 2015 they were protesting about garbage pickup. In 2019, they were united on a political front, and that was the difference.

Lebanon has been divided on a religious and political front for generations and to see the people rise against a 'corrupt' government, was beautiful to most outsiders looking in. This may be a sign of what is to come for a Lebanon that has stood divided for so long.

By 2020, the protests kept coming and the people were ready to see change. Even through the worldwide pandemic hit, COVID-19, the people were ready to act. A new government took shape after Saad Hariri stepped down. Again, the world was watching in anticipation of Lebanon turning the corner and becoming a state of equality and progress.

In the west, they wanted to see the people continue their protests until the necessary change came about. In a country where 10% of the people are considered elite, and 90% are considered poor, there is a ridiculously small middle class, if any. It is difficult to run a country this way. The Middle East is known for these types of governing ways that cause this circumstance.

If you look at history of countries with one supreme ruler, you'll find situations quite like what Lebanon has endured politically.

In Iraq, Saddam Hussein was the supreme leader for decades until he was ousted and captured. He owned countless presidential palaces and lived a life of luxury. All the while, millions of people in Iraq lived in poverty. Lebanon's poor class has never had to live through a supreme leader, thanks to the split government, but the idea is the same in terms of having many the population living in unfortunate circumstances.

Saddam Hussein earned worldwide attention in the early 1990s for nearly starting World War 3. Thankfully, that did not happen. For a time, it shifted attention away from Lebanon as it was the same time as the end of the civil war, and the west had a new person to hate.

Many countries in the Middle East are very conservative when it comes to religion. Many of these countries are dominated by people of Muslim faith, and as such, their rules are according to the Muslim faith. We have already talked about how Lebanon stands out due to its religious diversity. Moving forward, if they are united, that diversity can make Lebanon into a much stronger country.

With the protests happening and the new generation coming of age, Lebanon looked prime to move forward as a country that could soon realize its potential. Change was coming and the world could now see it. But then, August 4, 2020 happened. It was bad, it was worse than bad. It was tragic.

AUGUST 4, 2020

On this very day, an explosion rocked the country of Lebanon. In what was quite possibly the biggest non-nuclear explosion in history, the entire world watched as a senseless explosion hit the capital city in a docking port. Over 2700 tons of ammonium nitrate was being stored in this facility, and it was stored for over seven years!

How could this happen? The people of Lebanon have been through so much in the last 100 years, and they were about to go through more. Watching the first video that came out to mainstream media, you just could not believe what you were seeing. This tragedy was nothing short of horrifying.

People walking through the streets that day completely unsuspecting of what was about to happen. And just like in other circumstances the country has seen in the past, people waking up that morning and leaving their home, some of them did not return. It was almost as if we were watching a Hollywood movie.

As more videos came out onto mainstream media, we noticed that it was a tragedy far greater and far worse than we could've ever imagined. If you were a Lebanese person situated anywhere around the world, you were likely part of some sort of chat group on WhatsApp or maybe even Messenger, and you were witness to videos that showed you something that the world news would not show. Dead bodies lying in the streets, with their insides torn out, unsuspecting citizens going about their lives.

The people that were shooting these video frames were beside themselves, and completely overcome with emotion at the atrocity they were witnessing. It's hard to believe that something like this could happen, especially in modern day. And for anywhere in the entire world for this to happen, of all places, it happened in Beirut!

This explosion made international headlines for all the wrong reasons. For the first two weeks of August 2020, the entire world was talking about it. Sadly, it will eventually be a distant memory for all those that were not directly impacted. This serves as a reminder, that anything can happen in life, we just don't know. The people of Lebanon have gone through so much and as strong as they are, they will overcome this.

These are people that can overcome any obstacle the world will throw at them! They will not be defeated! They will not let circumstances like this put them down, because nothing will keep them down! The people of Lebanon have spent 100 years facing adversity and beating adversity! Life only defeats you when you let it, and you can ask any one person living in that country, more specifically living in

Beirut, and they will show you a resolve and human spirit within themselves that you will not see anywhere else in the world.

These people spend their lives fighting, they fight for each other, they fight for their loved ones, and they fight for their country. The recent economic collapse has been difficult on everyone. But these people maintain their strength and they are still proud citizens of this country. All the Lebanese people living around the world are still proud to call Lebanon home.

They jump at the chance to brag about how beautiful it is, how great the weather is, and how its like no other place on earth. They jump at the opportunity to go back and visit and spend time with the citizens and the people of this great country. The adversity and obstacles that Lebanon has faced in the last 100 years have tested this country time and again. That would defeat most people, and it would defeat other countries around the world, but the people of Lebanon will always rise above the tests that are put in front of them.

The strength of humanity will most often be seen in the face of difficulties. Life is not always sunshine; Life is what is put in front of you. If you were to walk through the streets of Lebanon on August 4, 2020, what you would've seen is something you would not have expected. Among all the carnage of what happened, it's all people helping each other, men and women getting their children to safety. People protecting each other, that is what humanity is all about!

Just like the 1970s and 1980s, where all you saw on the news was people fleeing from danger. Just like the war of 2006, when we saw a country decimated by war again. That war of 2006 took out bridges, took down buildings, and left the country in shambles. But it did not defeat the people! It did not break the people of Lebanon! You can throw anything you want at the people of this country and YOU WILL NOT BREAK THEM!

They have been through too much, over too long a period, to give up now. The irresponsibility of whomever was in charge, that led to this deadly explosion on August 4, 2020, is just unfathomable. The countless videos that we have watched all over the world in the time since the explosion, has shown us what really happened. It has shown us how people really did suffer, in the face of an explosion that just should not have happened!

Going forward, in the next 100 years, Lebanon will again be faced with more adversity. But again, they will rise above it like they always do! They will fight in the face of fear! They will let nothing destroy what they do have, and that is the human spirit. The human spirit can defeat all that comes against it.

Any true citizen of Lebanon will tell you this, they will not back down, ever. With the entire world that is watching now, take note, Lebanon will overcome like they always do. The greatest country in the world will always be Lebanon, not because of the attractions, not because of the weather and not because of the food. Lebanon is the greatest country in the world because of its people!

Beirut Burning, it may always be that way. But I am not talking about the infrastructure. I am talking about the people. Their hearts are burning. There is a fire within the soul of that city, a fire that will never be put out! In all it's strength and power, representing how strong its citizens are, that fire will burn forever.

THE FUTURE

The people of Lebanon will see a lot of change as the future becomes present. The country has overcome adversity in all phases, and it will continue to overcome. As the first 100 years ends, and the next 100 years await, the generations forthcoming will have a lot more pressure to sustain an environment that is fair and just.

The people that have run this country will no longer be around. People will die, and they will be replaced by people who will take on the responsibility of leadership. Nobody lives forever. If Lebanon can maintain its peace, then the generations forthcoming will have a much easier time to lead. The memories of the 1975-1990 civil war will fade away and the people living in future generations will not have much connection to their forefathers that died on the battle ground.

If you look at the world today, there is no living World War 1 veteran. They have all died and moved to heaven. The last living

World War 1 veteran died in 2012. That means there is no living connection in the entire world left from that phase of time, in terms of people that were on the battleground.

With no living connection left, the last link of World War 1 is now gone, and all that are left are memories and stories of how it was back then. The great-great grandchildren of those soldiers are living in present day, many of them never meeting their great-great grandfathers, the soldiers that survived the war.

A soldier that was 18 years old when he went to war but survived, may have died in the

1950s or even the 1960s. His great-great grandchildren may not have been born until the 1980s or 1990s. This new generation doesn't know the horrifying life of the past, of World War 1 and how that war decimated Europe at that time.

In the present, people travel the world and interact with one another. Descendants from countries of the Allied Powers interact with the descendants from countries of the Central Powers. Americans and Canadians interact with Germans and Bulgarians. The world has changed, the hate of that time is now gone. The fighting happened, and then the world moved on.

Lebanon is at a stage where it needs to move forward. After all that has happened, the civil war, the war of 2006, the economic meltdown, the 2020 explosion that shocked the world. Lebanon has future generations that need to move on, put the hate and disorganization in the past, and make the country the best it can be.

The Lebanon of the future will be unlike the Lebanon of the past. At some point before the year 2030, Lebanon will have a leader that will take the country to new heights and into prominence it has not seen in its history. At one-point heaven on earth, and at one-point hell on earth. The leader that comes forward and does right by the people, he will be loved and respected. His legacy will live on the next 100 years as the man who made change happen.

This is now the time for that leader to emerge. Lebanon has had countless leaders assassinated or pushed out of office due to public pressure amid corruption. The people need a man they can trust. The people need a man that will be their voice on a united front.

By the year 2100, there will be no living soldiers from the civil war of 1975-1990. There will only be stories in history books and schools teaching the students of how things were. The further we get away from that war, the more society in Lebanon will be able to move forward and the hate will dissipate.

But people don't want to wait until the end of this century to realize what Lebanon can be. They don't want to wait for change. Life is too short; they want that change now! That change is forthcoming. In other countries, although politicians are known for getting away with alleged corruption to some degree, eventually the truth comes to bare. But with the Lebanon of the past, the finger pointing doesn't stop.

The last chapter of this book talks about the August 4, 2020 explosion in Beirut. The most unfortunate circumstance of that entire situation is that people were killed and/or injured. Innocent people being affected is the worst possible scenario and it happened.

Behind the unfortunate death and injuries, there will be nobody taking responsibility for this. Not one person will spend a day in jail. Try explaining that to the families affected by this! Even worse, they all know that there will be nobody taking liability for this! It is a helpless situation.

Investigations will be done; people will be blamed. But let's be real about this, you know, and I know that it will not go further than an investigation. Everyone on earth knows that, not to mention the people of Lebanon.

The future does hold bright, now that the people are uniting and wanting a better life for all the people of Lebanon. Being united is the only way that change will occur and be sustained long-term. That country will flourish, and it will rise again. Beirut is a city like no other, in a country like no other. Lebanon is beautiful, and it always will be.

THE END